CASTLES

AND

FORTRESSES

CASTLES
AND
FORTRESSES

ROBIN S. OGGINS

Friedman Group

*𝔉ront cover: Neuschwanstein Castle, Bavaria, Germany. **Back cover:** Bodium Castle, East Sussex, England. **Page 2:** The Castle of Fenis, Val d'Aosta, Italy. **Page 5:** Château l'Aigle, Switzerland. **Page 6:** Egeskov Castle, island of Funen, Denmark.*

A FRIEDMAN GROUP BOOK

© 1994 by Michael Friedman Publishing Group, Inc.

Oggins, Robin S., 1931–
   Castles and Fortresses/Robin S.Oggins.
      p. cm.
   "Castles and Fortresses was prepared and produced by Michael Friedman Publishing Group, Inc."—T.p. verso.
   "A Friedman Group book"—T.p. verso.
   Includes bibliographical references and index.
   ISBN 1-56799-095-9
    1. Castles—History. 2. Architecture, Medieval.
  3. Fortification—History. I. Michael Friedman Publishing Group.
  II. Title.
NA7710.037 1994   94-9454
728.8'1'0902—dc20   CIP

CASTLES AND FORTRESSES
was prepared and produced by
Michael Friedman Publishing Group, Inc.
15 West 26th Street
New York, New York 10010

Editor: Benjamin Boyington
Art Director: Jeff Batzli
Designer: Lynne Yeamans
Layout: Philip Travisano
Photography Editor: Susan Mettler

Color separations by Bright Arts (H.K.) Ltd.
Printed and bound in China by Leefung-Asco Printers Ltd.

To Ginny, Jean, Cy, and Kathy,

who explored castles with me.

CONTENTS

———•◆•———

THE EVOLUTION OF THE CASTLE

Castles, broadly defined, can probably be traced back to prehistory. The word castle *is derived from the Latin* castrum, *a fortified military camp usually surrounded by a palisade and a ditch. However, a castle is most often associated with the western Middle Ages and is more strictly defined as a large fortified stronghold inhabited by a lord. A castle, if very elaborate, can be what is ordinarily called a palace; at the other end of the scale, a castle can be simply a fortified manor house. The castle is essentially a combination of military and domestic architecture—a place where the owner can find security from his enemies.*

The medieval castle originated in the ninth century in the Frankish Empire (what is now modern France, western Germany, and northern Italy) as nobles began building fortifications in response to increasing insecurity in the region. During much of the eighth century, the Franks were led by strongmen—Charles the Hammer (716–741), Pepin the Short (reigned 751–768), and Charlemagne (r. 768–814). In the ninth century, the quality of leadership declined: Charlemagne's son was known as Louis the Pious (r. 814–840), and Louis' descendants included Charles the Fat, Charles the Simple, and Lewis the Child. The Carolingians (Charlemagne's dynasty) divided their lands among royal heirs, and this custom led to a multiplicity of kings and to civil wars. The new institution of feudalism (which usually involved cavalry service in return for land—the fief—and political rights) resulted in an increase in lordships held under the kings. An intensifying series of attacks by Vikings and later in the century by Magyars (Hungarians) and by Arabs from North Africa made life in this period still more insecure. Political instability and invasion by outside forces resulted in a breakdown in law and order and a sharp decline in the effectiveness of central government. Consequently, power fell into the hands of whatever lords or strongmen were able to protect local populations effectively. But the strongmen also had to protect themselves, and the result was the building of defensive structures that over time evolved into castles.

One reason for the Vikings' success was that many of their targets lacked substantial defenses. By the mid-ninth century, however,

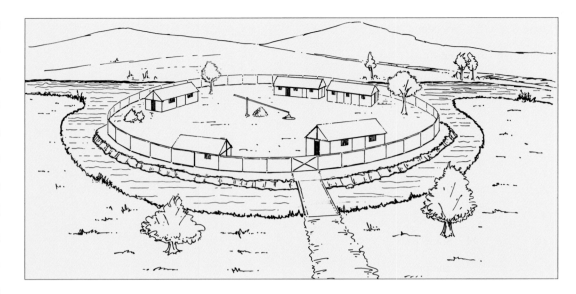

Page 8: *Conwy Castle, Gwynedd, northern Wales.* **Page 9:** *The Tower of London as depicted in a manuscript illustration from the* Poems of Charles d'Orléans, *late 15th century.* **Above:** *A reconstruction drawing of the Husterknupp, a late ninth-century fortified farmstead on the river Erft in West Germany. While the wall was made of wood, the diverted river served as a moat and the bridge could be drawn up to provide a refuge from Viking attacks. By the twelfth century, the Husterknupp was the site of a motte-and-bailey castle.*

———— ❖ ————

cities and monasteries in what is now France were building walls to protect themselves against Viking attack. At around the same time, lords began building fortifications to protect themselves from foreign invaders and from one another. In 862 the West Frankish king Charles the Bald (r. 840–877) issued the Edict of Pitres, which provided that fortifications might be built against the invaders. This edict had

unforeseen results: so many castles were built that two years later Charles had to issue another edict requiring destruction of castles built without royal permission. There is no real indication that this second edict was, or indeed could be, enforced.

These early "castles" were most likely built of wood. Often, no doubt, the fortifications amounted to little more than a wooden stockade around the lord's residence. Such defenses could be put up quickly, and their mere existence might cause invaders to bypass the stronghold. Such castles could also serve as a refuge for the neighboring population. But wooden walls certainly would not have held against a serious assault by invaders who by the late ninth century were attacking such fortified cities as Paris and London.

During the tenth century, there was a great increase in castle building in mainland western Europe. In northern Spain castles were built along frontiers with the Muslims, and in eastern Germany fortifications were built for protection from the local Wends and Slavs. In France castles were built by the more powerful nobles, such as the dukes of Normandy and the counts of Anjou, in order to consolidate their control over their territories and as protection against other nobles. Unlike the earlier castles, these structures were built to last longer and provide a more substantial defense. In general, these castle builders took advantage of the local terrain, building on high or relatively inaccessible sites, diverting rivers, and using earthworks whenever possible. Some early castles took the form of towers, but the prevailing form, first in France and later in England, came to be known as the "motte-and-bailey" castle. The motte was a high mound of earth (sometimes constructed by the builders) on which the lord's residence was placed. Placing the castle on higher ground increased the defenders' field of view and forced attackers to climb, slowing them down and making them more vulnerable to the defenders' weapons. The motte was surrounded by a wall or stockade and by a ditch that was sometimes filled with water. The bailey was a larger area—sometimes 5 acres (2ha) or more—adjacent to the motte. Within the bailey were residential buildings, storage sheds, barns, and other secondary structures. The bailey was also protected by a wall, and the whole castle area was typically surrounded by another ditch (the "moat").

In the beginning, therefore, castles were constructed as refuges. Initially, the lord's main concern was to fortify his residence as quickly as possible. However, as enemies changed from hit-and-run invaders to neighboring lords, a need developed for stronger castles that could withstand sieges. By the late tenth century, some castles were being built of stone, and some motte-and-bailey castles had been rebuilt

Top: An example of a castle sited especially to take advantage of the terrain for defense. Illustration from the Bellifortis Manuscript, Italian, 15th century. Above: After being set on fire, Conan of Britanny's wooden motte-and-bailey castle at Dinan surrenders to William, Duke of Normandy. Detail of the Bayeux Tapestry, English, c. 1067–1077.

using this material. Building in stone was more expensive and took much longer than building in wood, and local stone was used whenever possible—this is one reason castles in different geological regions look different from one another. Stone for construction was sometimes brought from a distance: the Tower of London, for example, was built of white stone shipped from Caen in Normandy. The Bayeux Tapestry illustrates one reason for building in stone: one section shows Duke Conan of Brittany's castle at Dinan being set afire by Duke William of Normandy's soldiers.

By the late eleventh century and during the twelfth, new castles were often built in the form of rectangular stone towers (keeps). The most famous of these is the White Tower—the original Tower of London and now the central structure of the Tower complex—which was begun around 1078 to replace an earlier fortress built in 1066. The great keeps were too heavy to be raised on artificial mounds of earth, but earthworks or exterior fences were still used to provide additional protection. Access to the aboveground entry to the keep was typically provided by a wooden stair that could be removed in case of a siege.

Over time, castles evolved in response to developments in siege machinery and siege-craft. However, as castles became more elaborate, they also became more expensive, and fewer and fewer lords could afford fortresses that were militarily up to date. A major problem with square tower keeps (such as Hedingham, p. 23) was that they were vulnerable to attack from the corners. While defenders could fire on besiegers through arrow slits or drop objects on attackers from above, if the besiegers could get to a corner of the keep, they could work away at the base of the wall with picks; eventually, the attackers would in this way either break through the wall or cause it to collapse by undermining the corner. During the twelfth and thirteenth centuries, castle builders developed several answers to this problem. Circular keeps were built, as at Restormel, thus eliminating the vulnerable corners. At Dover and elsewhere, stone walls with projecting towers were built to surround the square keep; these towers provided a vantage point from which archers defending the castle could shoot at enemies along the base of the wall.

To hold out against a siege required a protected water supply—generally a well—and enough stored food to keep the defenders from being starved out. In any given case, the length of time a siege might last depended also on other factors. When an army moved into enemy territory, its forces were reduced each time its leader detached men to besiege a castle. In a hostile area with many castles, the besieger was liable to be besieged by relief forces who could pin the attackers down. There was always the danger of disease breaking out in a besieging camp. Weather and the instability of the besieging force could be factors in the duration of a siege; in the eleventh and twelfth centuries, campaigns were generally undertaken in the summer, and feudal military service was usually limited to forty days, placing limits on the length of most sieges.

From the point of view of the besieger, it was important both militarily and psychologically that enemy castles be taken as quickly as

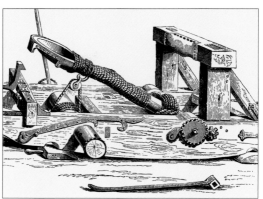

Top: Depiction of a siege of a square keep. Note the man with the pick working away at the base of the castle. Also note the women taking an active part in the castle's defense. Illustration from the Manesse Manuscript, German, c. 1300–1340. Above: Reconstruction drawing of a mangonel.

possible. Occasionally a castle could be taken by surprise or by storm. Sometimes the defenders assessed the besieging forces and negotiated a surrender, hoping they would get better terms before the siege than they would afterward. Garrisons that held out might be massacred after their surrender. Sometimes everyone in the castle was killed; sometimes the women were spared. At one siege of the Husterknupp in Germany, the women were allowed to leave with whatever they could take away; they emerged carrying their husbands on their shoulders.

In addition to military coercion, besiegers might apply psychological pressure to bring about a surrender. When John Marshal refused to surrender his castle at Newbury to King Stephen (r. 1135–1154), the king threatened to hang John's son, the child William Marshal, whom the king held as hostage for John's good behavior. John, remarking that he could have other sons, still refused to surrender. King Stephen relented and later blocked a plan to catapult William into the castle. On other occasions, hostages were not as fortunate. Treachery was another expedient used to take castles. Some besiegers broke truces or attacked on holy days. In 1098 the soldiers of the First Crusade (1096–1099) were let into Antioch by a man who had earlier been forcibly converted to Islam.

When such expedients failed, siege engines could be employed. These included several kinds of long-range, projectile-throwing machines: the medieval catapult or ballista took the form of a giant crossbow; the mangonel held a missile in a cup and was wound up like a

*Left: Reconstruction drawing of a siege tower. **Right:** Reconstruction drawing of a battering ram.*

a 95-foot (29m) tower was used. A battering ram—sometimes a tree trunk capped with an iron point—could be used to break through the gates of the castle. A wooden shed covered with wet hides could be used to protect the attackers, with the ram hung by chains from the roof beam of the shed. At times as many as sixty men were used to swing a battering ram.

Mining was another technique used to destroy castle walls: attackers would dig a tunnel under the castle wall, propping up the base of the wall with wooden beams. When the tunnel had been dug far enough beneath the wall, the beams would be set on fire, causing the section of the wall above the mine to collapse. Sometimes defenders built their own tunnels to flood those created by the attackers. At the siege of St. Andrews Castle, Scotland (1546–1547), the attackers dug a tunnel 6 feet (1.8m) wide and 7 feet (2.1m) high through rock in an attempt to undermine the Fore Tower. The defenders, in turn, dug their own mine, and an underground battle was fought between the two teams of diggers. Needless to say, sieges combined all these techniques and added others, such as firing incendiary arrows in the hope of starting fires within the castle.

The castle builders' response to these various kinds of attack was to reinforce the exterior castle defenses. During the late twelfth and thirteenth centuries, earthworks were replaced by

sling and so powered by torsion; the trebuchet consisted of a sling powered by a counterweight. These devices could be used to propel a variety of missiles, including the heads of enemies, dead animals, cartloads of manure, pots of fire, and very large stones. One fourteenth-century military treatise even contains an illustration of a machine for throwing beehives into a fortress. In 1188, the Muslim military leader Saladin (r. 1174–1193) used stone balls said to weigh up to 600 pounds (272kg) to demolish the walls of the Crusader castle of Saône.

When attackers could fill the moat and get close to the castle walls, other devices could be used. Wheeled towers would be brought up to a castle wall and a hinged platform at the tower's top lowered onto the wall; the besiegers would climb ladders inside the towers and cross to the wall. Such siege towers were made of wood, and to prevent their being set on fire by the defenders, the towers were often covered with wet hides. At the siege of Lisbon in 1147,

stone walls, and access to castles was made more difficult by use of both natural and man-made barriers. One such barrier was a heavily fortified outer tower (barbican) situated in front of the original gatehouse. Moats were built, and drawbridges that could be drawn up or destroyed were used to cross them; sometimes, as at Bodiam Castle, there were several drawbridges, based on small islets, to be crossed. Castle gates were reinforced by a heavy iron grille (the portcullis), and often several of these had to be passed before one could enter the castle interior.

During the Crusades, which began in the late eleventh century, western forces encountered Byzantine and Arabic fortifications, which were more sophisticated than the castles they had previously been familiar with. When Richard "the Lion Heart" of England (r. 1189–1199) returned to his domains after the Third Crusade and his subsequent imprisonment in Germany, he built Château Gaillard, a castle on the river Seine near Les Andelys in Normandy, which is usually considered one of the earliest castles built using principles of fortification learned on crusade. The work was completed in two years. Château Gaillard was part of a broader defensive scheme, including fortifications on the river, that was designed to prevent the king of France from using the Seine to attack the Norman capital of Rouen. The castle itself was on a steep bluff overlooking the river and could only be approached from one direction. To take the castle, attackers would have to capture a fortified outer bailey, cross a narrow bridge, and then take, in succession, a middle bailey, an inner bailey, and finally the great round tower (donjon). The castle seemed impregnable, yet it fell in 1204 to King Philip Augustus of France (r. 1179–1223) after a siege of only six months. The tower at the apex of the walls was mined and the outer bailey taken.

en mille chose de ce monde ne se pourroit trouuer/mais chascun de nous le cognoist tard/et apres ce que en a uons eu besoing. Toutes fois vault encores myeulx tard que samais

Sensuyt le commencement des guerres qui furent entre le duc de bourgongne et les liegeoys.

insi se passeret aucunes anees durant lesqlles le duc de bour gongne auoit guerre chas cun an auecques les liege oys. Quant le Roy le veoit empesche/il essavoit a faire quelque nouueaul te contre les bretons / en faisant quelque peu de confort aux liegeoys.

Left: Reconstruction drawing of the 1204 siege of Château Gaillard. Above: Illustration of cannon at a siege from the Memoirs of Philippe de Commynes, *Rouen, France, 16th century.*

Richard's builders had made several mistakes: the bridge between the outer and middle baileys was fixed, and French engineers were able to shelter under it and mine the walls of the middle bailey; the builders had also built a latrine (garderobe) discharge shaft within the walls, and the French climbed up the shaft and took the middle bailey gate. Eventually, the remainder of the castle was taken by storm.

During the thirteenth century, in response to the use of more powerful siege weapons, castle builders concentrated on extending and strengthening outer defenses. Often this involved building an outer wall that was lower than the inner one. The outer wall served as a first line of defense, but would itself be subject to fire from the defenders on the inner wall if the outer wall was captured. Since the weakest part of a castle wall was its entrance, flanking towers were built to provide broad fields of fire, enabling defenders to protect castle gateways. The castle gatehouse was fortified more and more strongly until gatehouses themselves became virtual castles. Builders everywhere tried to create castles that could continue to hold out even when large portions of them had been taken by an enemy. Perhaps the best examples of thirteenth-century castle building are the series of castles built by King Edward I of England (r. 1272–1307) as part of his conquest of North Wales. These castles—Aberystwyth, Beaumaris (p. 47), Builth, Caernarvon (p. 20), Conwy (pp. 18–19), Flint, Harlech (p. 46), and Rhuddlan—were all begun between 1277 and 1295; six of them were directly associated with new towns built by Edward. Taken as a group, these fortifications represent castles at the peak of the evolutionary process of castle building.

Because of the generally unsettled nature of the times, the fourteenth and fifteenth centuries saw a great increase in the number of castles built. From the standpoint of castle building, the single most important development of this period was the institution of artillery. By the 1330s cannon were being used in warfare, and by the end of the fourteenth century, they were playing an increasingly important role in sieges. At first, cannon tended to be very large; some fired stone balls weighing more than 500 pounds (227kg) and had to be carried in carts from place to place. By the mid-fifteenth century, cannon were being mounted on wheels and could be moved more freely. Smaller guns also came into use around this time, and gun ports were built in castle walls so the defenders could use their own firearms against besiegers. In the long run, however, the new developments favored the besiegers. Castles continued to resist sieges into the seventeenth century, but eventually most were battered into ruins.

During the fourteenth and fifteenth centuries, there was also a growing tendency for

——◆——

Below: Deal Castle, Kent, England, was built by King Henry VIII in 1539 as an artillery castle that was part of a coastal defense system.

great nobles throughout Europe to build magnificent residences. Some of these nobles maintained private armies dressed in uniforms (liveries), and their houses were to some degree built for defensive purposes. The main purpose of these castles, however, was to serve as public displays of the importance of the people who lived in them. In this respect, such late-medieval castles represent a transitional phase between the fortresses of the past and the great houses of the postmedieval period. While these fourteenth- and fifteenth-century castles retained a military appearance with stone walls and crenellations, they were designed more for the physical comfort of their owners than for defensive capabilities. In the sixteenth century and after, fortified structures continued to be built. King Henry VIII of England (r. 1509–1547) built a series of coastal defenses, including Deal Castle, against possible invaders. These castles, however, were not residences for the owner, and they therefore mark the beginning of a new era in military fortification.

Right: Château Gaillard, Les Andelys (Eure), France, was built by King Richard "the Lion Heart" of England between 1196 and 1198.

Left: Conwy Castle, Gwynedd, northern Wales, was built and largely completed by Edward I of England between 1283 and 1287.

op: Caernarvon Castle, Gwynedd, northern Wales, was begun by Edward I of England in 1283, and building continued until at least 1323.

*Above: Interior view of Caernarvon Castle. **Right:** Restormel Castle, Cornwall, England. Though the castle was founded around 1100, the ring wall dates from c. 1200.*

Left: Dover Castle, Kent, England, is one of the few castles in England that may have been founded before the Norman Conquest. The present castle was begun by King Henry II around 1167 and additions have been made ever since—most recently during the Second World War. *Top:* View of the ramparts at Dover Castle. *Above:* Hedingham Castle, Essex, England, built 1130 to 1140.

THE SITING OF CASTLES AND THE EVOLUTION OF CASTLE INTERIORS

While security was the main purpose of most castles, they

might have served other important functions as well.

Castles were often built to control a given area; they might

be placed at strategic locations to control transportation

routes or to facilitate the collection of tolls on such routes.

Some castles were put in the middle of towns or at their

edges—both to dominate the town and to provide protec-

tion for the lord against a potentially rebellious citizenry.

Other castles were built in isolated areas as refuges. A

castle's purpose generally influenced its construction as well

as its location. Castles designed as refuges for local popula-

tions had to be made large enough to hold the people to be sheltered. Castle builders usually tried to take advantage of features in the terrain to reinforce the castle's defenses. When natural defensive features were not available, as in the case of a castle built in the middle of a city, the builders had to compensate in other ways—for instance, by building an elaborate moat.

Castles almost always served as local governmental centers—as the site of the lord's court and of his manorial administration. While a direct relationship generally existed between the wealth and importance of the lord and the size of the castle, this was not simply because the castle was a status symbol. Great nobles had large households and retinues and often had to entertain guests with similar followings. A castle had to be large enough to house at least the more important retainers of the lord and his guests, even though it might remain largely unoccupied for much of the year as its lord traveled elsewhere. Castles might also have nonresidential purposes; the Tower of London, for example, was the site of a royal treasury and a royal mint, and later became an important prison, as well as the site of the royal zoo. Whenever castles assumed such nondefensive functions, additional space had to be found or built in. Interior defensibility, as well as protection from exterior threats, also affected a castle's construction. During the fourteenth and fifteenth centuries, many lords' retinues were composed of mercenary soldiers who might be bribed to change allegiance. New kinds of interior security were therefore needed. Late-medieval castle builders often restricted access to parts of the castle by such means as draw-

bars, or by building the castle in such a way that the garrison was housed at some distance from the lord and would have to pass through a courtyard to get to his living quarters.

Medieval castles were not particularly comfortable places in which to live. Because they were built for defense, they tended to be dark and claustrophobic. In early castles, arrow slits were the main sources of natural light, and because these openings were narrow, so that castle archers did not become targets for

A *bove: Arrow slits in the curtain walls of Krak des Chevaliers in Syria. The arched embrasures and the battlements enabled archers to reload safely before firing through the arrow slits.*

attackers, the slits did not provide much in the way of light. Lighting was also provided by candles, torches, or oil lamps—smoky, dim, and flickering at worst, and at best, still far below modern standards of illumination. Staircases were built within the thickness of the wall and were deliberately narrow so that the defenders would face only one attacker at a time; needless to say, darkness and the narrowness of both stairway and tread could make going up and down difficult and even dangerous for the castle's residents. Privies were also built within the walls, with chutes to carry human waste outside the castle or into the moat.

Castles were generally cold and drafty. In early castles, heat was often provided by an open hearth, with some of the smoke escaping through a hole in the roof. Later, fireplaces were introduced, and while they were certainly an improvement over the central hearth, they did not provide much heat for those of the lord's retainers who were of lower rank and whose places were far from the fire.

The most important and largest room in the castle was the great hall. This room served as the official center of the castle, where court was held, guests were entertained, and the members of the household ate their meals. One should think of the hall as a center for a range of diverse activities where at the same time the lord might be dining, musicians playing, and dogs being fed and falcons trained. The lord, his

Left: Garderobe discharge chutes, Greencastle, County Down, Northern Ireland. This keep was built in the mid-thirteenth century. Above: A lord at dinner; note the great number of retainers. Illustration for the month of January from the Grimani Breviary *(Flemish, c. 1480–1520).*

immediate family, and his guests would sit at a high table that might be set on a raised platform or dais. The lord might be further set apart by being seated in a chair, while everyone else sat on benches or stools. In the early Middle Ages, the hall was also where the household slept, with the lord and his family perhaps separated from the rest of the household by a screen. By the thirteenth century, the more wealthy began to use tapestries to control drafts and to provide some insulation against the cold of stone walls. Rushes or grasses and fragrant herbs were scattered on the floor to absorb the household litter. Later, rushes came to be replaced by rugs.

In time, the upper part of the hall—the lord's "great chamber"—came to be closed off. In this chamber, the lord could eat and sleep apart from most of his household. The great chamber evolved into what might be called the lord's personal public space—a living room rather than a retreat. By the thirteenth century, a desire for privacy led to the building of separate private chambers for the lord and his family. When these rooms were built on an upper floor and lit (and warmed) by sunlight, they were called solars.

Other important parts of the castle included the chapel, which could be very elaborate, and the service quarters. The latter included the kitchens, the pantry, the wine cellar, sometimes a separate brewhouse, a laundry, and the storerooms used to keep provisions, fuel, and the payments in grain, animals, and the like made by the lord's tenants. Quarters were provided for the household and garrison, and stables for the horses of the lord, his retainers, and his guests were also provided.

As the Middle Ages progressed, lords began to spend more time in favored residences, rather than traveling from castle to castle. The growing emphasis on comfort in living was manifested in better and more elaborate furniture, since furnishings were no longer routinely carried from castle to castle. Trestle tables were replaced by dining tables; beds became more elaborate, with hangings to keep out the cold; and chests for storage were replaced by dressers and cabinets. More light was let into the living areas as arrow slits were enlarged and windows added, and with the introduction of glass in windows castles were more easily warmed and became less drafty. Landscape gardens began to be constructed on the castle grounds. In time, the castle was transformed into a palace or a great house.

*Above: The unicorn tries to escape. Detail of the third Unicorn Tapestry (Franco-Flemish, c. 1500). This tapestry is now in the possession of The Cloisters, a museum of medieval art and architecture in New York City featuring material from monastic ruins and buildings of southern France and Spain. **Left:** A medieval bedroom; again, note the number of attendants. Clearly, privacy in the Middle Ages was not what we regard as privacy today. The birth of Saint Edmund, from Lydgate,* The Life of St. Edmund; *Bury St. Edmund, after 1433.*

Left: The Great Hall of Berkeley Castle, Gloucestershire, England. Berkeley Castle was begun shortly after 1067, but the entire interior, including the Great Hall, was remodeled in the mid-fourteenth century. The screen at the end of the hall stands in front of passages to the kitchen and bakehouse. Above: Slit windows, Edinburgh Castle. Right: Modern windows, Edinburgh Castle.

Right: A narrow interior passage in the Tower of London. **Below:** A great chamber, Château d'Antony, France.

A *bove: Corfe Castle, Dorset, in southern England, was begun in the eleventh century. The word* corfen *is Old English for "cut" or "gap"—Corfe Castle is located atop a small hill in a gap in the Purbeck Hills. The castle guards the land access to the peninsula called the Isle of Purbeck.*

Opposite: Quéribus (Aude), in southern France, was the last Cathar retreat in France (the Cathars were a European heretical sect of the eleventh through the thirteenth centuries). It finally fell to Raymond VII, Count of Toulouse, in 1255. **Above:** *Puylaurens (Tarn), in southern France, was a stronghold of Cathar heretics in Languedoc during the thirteenth-century Albigensian Crusade.*

Left: The Gravensteen is a moated castle built in the middle of the city of Ghent, Belgium. It was begun in the ninth century, was destroyed in the early twelfth century, and starting in 1180 was rebuilt by Baldwin of Flanders. During the later Middle Ages, the Gravensteen was one of the residences of the counts of Flanders. The castle was restored early in the twentieth century.

Right: Loarre Castle, in Huesca Province in northern Spain, was built toward the end of the eleventh century. Note how it dominates the plain beyond it.

CHAPTER **III**

𝔊REAT 𝔅RITAIN AND 𝔍RELAND

With the Norman invasion came the reintroduction of stone

fortifications to England. The Romans had built stone forts

along Hadrian's Wall, a series of large stone "castles"

known as the Forts of the Saxon Shore along the southern

and eastern coasts of England, and also some stone city

walls (notably London Wall). The Anglo-Saxons used some

of these Roman structures, but their own buildings were

timber with earthworks. When Edward the Confessor

(r. 1042–1066) became King of England after a youth

spent in Normandy, he brought Norman advisors back

with him. These Normans introduced the stone castle

into England, although the number of such castles built under Edward was very small. But the Norman Conquest, led by Duke William "the Conqueror" of Normandy (r. 1066–1087), brought the building of stone castles on a large scale to the British Isles.

Although William defeated and killed King Harold II (r. 1066) and most of the Anglo-Saxon nobles at Hastings in October 1066, it took five more years to complete the Conquest. Rebellions, murders of individual Normans, and threats of invasion from Scandinavia continued to create problems for William until the end of his reign. The fact that William, like all succeeding English kings up to around 1200, spent less than half his reign in England complicated the situation. Because he regarded England as a provider of resources for his ventures in France, it was important that England be stabilized and the English be kept under control. The castle was one of the major elements of William's plan. A network of royal castles was built at strategic locations throughout England, both in the major towns and along the areas subject to invasion—the eastern coast and the Welsh and Scottish frontiers. These castles were supplemented by baronial castles, which also provided the Norman lords with protection from a hostile population.

In the early years of the Norman Conquest, the castles were generally of the wooden motte-and-bailey variety, such as the castle that was built at Hastings shortly after the Norman landing, because such castles could be built quickly. As time passed and the Conquest was consolidated, the castles of the king and of the greater nobles were rebuilt in stone, many on an

Page 38: One of the most beautiful of surviving medieval castles, Bodiam Castle, in East Sussex, England, was built in the mid-1380s, after a decade in which the French attacked and burned the nearby ports of Rye and Winchelsea and the Peasants' Revolt (1381) shook the established order. Bodiam's outer dimensions are 152 by 138 feet (46.3 by 42.1m), its walls are 6$^{1/2}$ feet (2m) thick at the base, and its towers rise more than 60 feet (18.3m) above the moat. Now in the care of the National Trust, Bodiam is not easy to get to but is well worth the trip. Page 39: Warwick Castle, Warwickshire, England, was founded in 1068 and was rebuilt and updated a number of times. Today it combines castle ruins, largely of the fourteenth century, with one of the finest great houses in England. The two small projecting towers, which date to the late fifteenth century, are said to have been built as artillery platforms. Note the landscaped park below the towers.

unprecedented scale. These new stone castles served a psychological function as well as a strategic one. They soared above the houses of the natives—the Tower of London was 90 feet (27.4m) high, the keep at Rochester 125 feet (38.1m)—and the sight of them constantly reminded the Anglo-Saxons of the power and authority of their Norman conquerors.

William I and his immediate successors, William II (r. 1087–1100) and Henry I (r. 1100–1135), kept general control over who built castles. But when Henry I died in 1135, leaving his daughter Matilda as his heir, civil war broke out. A woman had never before ruled England in her own right, and Matilda's cousin Stephen of Blois crossed the English Channel and claimed the crown. The resulting nineteen-year period of civil war is known as The Anarchy. With no effective central government in control, local magnates built castles by the hundreds. Finally in 1153 a compromise was worked out between the two claimants to the throne: Stephen was recognized as king but he was to be succeeded by Matilda's son, Henry II Plantagenet (r. 1154–1189).

Henry's first task was the restoration of order, and this meant demolishing the "adulterine" castles (those built without royal permission). Many of these strongholds were built of wood and were quickly destroyed, but throughout Henry's reign and those of his sons Richard I "the Lion Heart" and John (r. 1199–1216), there was a continuing policy of confiscating or destroying the castles of rebellious nobles while building new royal castles and strengthening older ones—Henry II's transformation of Dover Castle belongs to this period. It is worth remembering that many castles changed substantially over long periods of time, and that at very old castle sites, such as Leeds (p. 44), the surviving buildings may have been built centuries after the castle was originally founded.

Castles built during the twelfth century continued to be primarily rectangular tower keeps such as the Tower of London and the keep at Goodrich (p. 43). In the thirteenth century, wooden and earthwork outer defenses came to be replaced by stone, round keeps were built instead of square ones (as at Pembroke, p. 46), and central towers were augmented or replaced by circular or polygonal "curtain walls" with round projecting towers.

By the end of the thirteenth century, the prevailing type of new castle was the concentric castle—an exterior ring of walls, the "shell keep," often with no central tower (as at Restormel, pp. 20–21). The entrances to these castles (relative weak points) were first strengthened and later turned into massive gatehouses that could be defended even after the rest of the castle had been captured. One feature of these castles was the concentration of firepower so as to expose attackers to maximum assault by defenders. Firepower could be maximized by controlling access—attackers could be forced to approach a castle parallel to the walls via a right-angle bridge across a moat, as at Bodiam—or by building high towers that commanded not only the ground in front of the castle but the outside walls as well. The finest concentric castles were those built by Edward I in Wales—Beaumaris (p.47), Caernarvon, Conwy, and Harlech (p.46)—but smaller, later versions, such as Bodiam, are also noteworthy.

As castles became more elaborate and more expensive to build, only the great or the wealthy could afford them. Lesser nobles built fortified manor houses, often protected by moats, like Hever Castle (p. 42). Such houses could serve as protection during local insurrections or feuds, but would not be adequate in case of a serious siege. By the fifteenth century, the introduction of cannon had transformed siegecraft, and while new castles, such as Tattershall (p.45), continued to be built for defensive purposes, they also served to emphasize the social importance of the owner.

The castle in Scotland derived from English models. As in England, there were important royal castle-residences such as Stirling (p. 48), and Craigmillar (p. 51). Other castles, particularly in the Highlands, were the homes of clan chiefs, as in the cases of Castle Stalker (p. 48) and Dunvegan (pp. 52–53). From the four-

teenth century on, many of the fortified structures along the English-Scottish border were "tower houses," stone towers much like the Norman keep in which the entrance was often reached by a ladder or by a retractable stair that could be pulled up in time of danger. Inside, the tower houses were built so that attackers could take only one story at a time while being exposed to constant fire from the story above.

The Normans brought stone castles to Ireland in the latter part of the twelfth century. The Anglo-Norman invaders were faced with some of the same problems in controlling territory in Ireland that their Norman ancestors had faced in England, and the stone castle played an important role in the Anglo-Norman conquest of Ireland. Unlike England, however, Ireland was never completely conquered during the Middle Ages, and local Irish lords built stone castles of their own, such as Blarney Castle (p. 53).

Below: Sited within Portsmouth Harbor, about 3 miles (4.8km) east of Fareham, Hampshire, England, Portchester Castle consists of a twelfth-century castle with a Norman keep built into the corner of a Roman fort of the Saxon Shore. The Roman walls also enclose a Norman church.

Right: Found about 9 miles (14.4km) northwest of Royal Tunbridge Wells, Kent, England, Hever Castle is really a moated and fortified manor house. Although Hever was begun in the late twelfth century, its fortifications were largely built in the fourteenth century, during the period of French raids and the Peasants' Revolt; the surviving buildings date from the fifteenth and sixteenth centuries. Hever was the childhood home of Henry VIII's second queen, Anne Boleyn (1507–1536).

Above: Goodrich Castle, built above the river Wye in Herefordshire, England, was an important Welsh border castle during the twelfth and thirteenth centuries. The earliest surviving building is the square keep, built in the mid-twelfth century. During the thirteenth century, the keep was surrounded by stone walls. Around 1300 the castle was largely reconstructed and three large, round towers and a towered gatehouse were added. Goodrich is an excellent example of the ways in which a castle at a strategic location was modified a number of times to keep up with contemporary military developments.

A **bove:** *Leeds Castle, located in the town of Leeds, England, about 5 miles (8km) southwest of Maidstone, Kent, is built on two islands in an artificial lake and is a kind of aquatic motte-and-bailey. Probably begun in the eleventh century, Leeds was rebuilt in the thirteenth century and given additional water defenses in the fourteenth century. Leeds was a dower castle of Catherine of Valois (1401–1437), queen to Henry V (r. 1413–1422); their linked initials can be found in the wall and bed hangings of the Queen's Room.*

Left, top: Tattershall Castle in Lincolnshire, England, was built between 1434 and 1445 by Ralph Lord Cromwell, Treasurer for Henry VI (r. 1422–1461, 1470–1471), on the site of a thirteenth-century castle. The magnificent 110-foot-high (33.5m) tower is one of the finest pieces of brickwork in England. Erected for defense at a troubled time in English history, Tattershall is also a splendid statement of the prestige and wealth of its builder.

Left, bottom: *Tintagel, located on the northern coast of Cornwall, England, is said to have been one of King Arthur's residences. In fact, the remains there date from the twelfth and thirteenth centuries, hundreds of years after Arthur supposedly reigned. The desolate but impressive ruins, which cover both a rocky peninsula and part of the neighboring mainland, are reached only after a steep climb.*

Left: Pembroke Castle was built on an inlet of the sea in southwestern Wales and later became important as a base for English campaigns in Ireland. The oldest surviving structures are the 75-foot-high (22.9m) circular keep and the inner ward, built around 1200 by William Marshal, Earl of Pembroke and later Regent of England. The remainder of the castle was built during the thirteenth century. King Henry VII (r. 1485–1509) was born here, and the castle was in use as late as 1648, when it was surrendered to Oliver Cromwell (1599–1658).

Right: Harlech Castle, which overlooks the sea in northwestern Wales, was built by Edward I of England as part of his plan for controlling the Welsh. Probably begun in 1285 and largely completed in five years, Harlech is an outstanding example of the concentric castle. Its strong point is its massive four-towered gatehouse, which measures 80 by 54 feet (24.4 by 16.5m). Originally measuring 8 to 12$^{1}/_{2}$ feet (2.4 to 3.8m) thick, Harlech's curtain walls were later reinforced. Its strategic position made a moat necessary only on the eastern and southern sides.

Above: Beaumaris Castle, on the island of Anglesey just off the northwest coast of Wales, was begun in 1295 and was the eighth and last of the great castles built by Edward I of England to consolidate his conquest of North Wales. Left partially incomplete after the 1320s, Beaumaris has two great gatehouses, a moat, and an elaborate system of fortifications with the inner defenses commanding the curtain wall. Each interior section was built so it could be defended separately even if the rest of the castle had been taken. Beaumaris is considered the finest example of a concentric castle. **Right:** View from a turret showing the moat and the field of fire.

Above: *Located in southern Scotland between Glasgow and Edinburgh, Stirling Castle stands high on a rock dominating the road to the Highlands. Its strategic importance led to innumerable sieges and battles, including the Battle of Bannockburn (1314), fought 3 miles (4.8km) away from the castle, in which the Scots under Robert Bruce (r. 1306–1329) won independence from England. The present castle and palace date mainly from the fifteenth and sixteenth centuries, when Stirling was an important Stuart royal residence.* **Right:** *Castle Stalker, on an island in Loch Linnhe in the Scottish Highlands, was built in the mid-fifteenth century by the Stewarts of Appin to receive King James IV (r. 1488–1513). Now privately owned, it is essentially a restored tower house. Stalker was used as the French-held castle in* Monty Python and the Holy Grail.

Left: Eilean Donan Castle, in Ross and Cromarty in northwestern Scotland, was built in 1230 on a rocky islet at the confluence of Loch Ailsh, Loch Long, and Loch Duich. Eilean Donan was long a fortress of the Macraes. In 1719, Spanish troops were landed at the castle as part of an attempt to restore the Stuart dynasty to the British throne. The castle was shelled by a British warship and largely destroyed. Eilean Donan was restored in the twentieth century. ***Above:*** *Four miles (6.4km) south of Edinburgh, Craigmillar Castle was one of the favorite residences of Mary, Queen of Scots* (r. 1542–1587). The L-shaped great central tower, roughly 53 by 49 feet (16.2 by 14.9m), was built around 1375; the quadrangular wall with round towers was constructed some fifty years later. Craigmillar was one of the earliest castles in Scotland to be built with gun ports for cannon.

Left: Situated on the Isle of Skye off northwestern Scotland, Dunvegan Castle is the seat of the Clan MacLeod. While the original castle was probably built in the twelfth century, the present buildings are from the fourteenth century and later, with some reconstruction during the Victorian era. Dunvegan was formerly accessible only by boat. One of its most notorious features is the infamous "bottle dungeon" in which prisoners were thrown to drown. ***Above and right:*** Located 6 miles (9.6m) from Cork in southern Ireland, Blarney Castle was built in 1446 by Cormac McCarthy. Its massive keep is 89 feet (27.1m) high, and at some points its walls are 18 feet (5.5m) thick. The Blarney Stone, a rock located just below the battlements, is said to make eloquent anyone who kisses it.

C H A P T E R IV

𝔉 R A N C E ,

𝔖 P A I N ,

A N D

𝔍 T A L Y

French castles were among the earliest to evolve. Until the

late twelfth century, France was ruled by weak kings, and

feudal France was composed largely of territories ruled over

by great nobles. In territories where the nobles were strong

(such as the Duchy of Normandy), the lords exerted some

control over castle building. In other areas, such as south-

ern France, every lord had his castle. During the eleventh

and twelfth centuries, the great lords (including the kings

of France) built stone castles to control the main roads

through their territories. They gave control of these castles

to royal servants (castellans), not all of whom proved to be trustworthy; as a result, nobles sometimes had to recapture their own castles. Castles played a significant role in the long-term conflicts between the kings of England and France—as in the case of Château Gaillard (p. 14 and pp. 16–17). In the fourteenth and fifteenth centuries, when the Hundred Years' War (1337–1453) was fought mostly on French territory, the number of French castles built increased substantially. By the late fifteenth century, castles in France (as elsewhere) were built largely for comfort and conspicuous display, culminating in the magnificent Renaissance castles of the Loire Valley.

Page 54: The Château of Angers (Maine-et-Loire) in western France was constructed between 1228 and 1238. Built in the shape of a pentagon, Angers once had seventeen flanking towers, and the perimeter of its wall was more than half a mile (0.8m) long. The decorative patterns of Angers' stone courses are striking. **Page 55:** *Located in an area of Normandy once much disputed between*

English and French kings, the Château of Gisors was begun by King William II of England in 1097. In the second half of the twelfth century, Henry II, King of England and Duke of Normandy, expanded Gisors, surrounding the keep with a polygonal wall with nine flanking towers. Gisors is a fine example of a strategically located castle modified to keep up with developing military strategy.

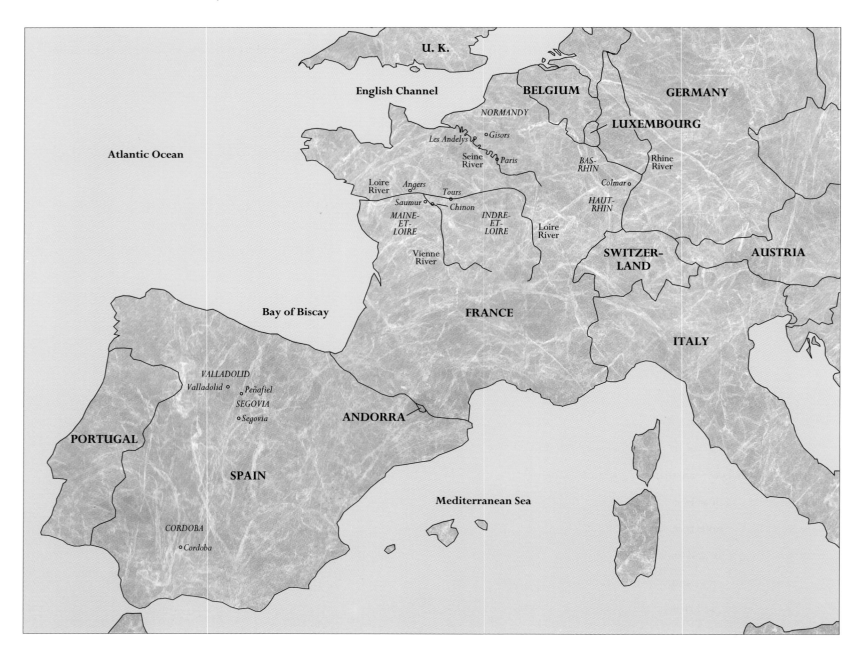

In Spain, the development of castles was conditioned by the *Reconquista*, the reconquest of Spain from the Arabs from the tenth century to 1492, when the troops of Ferdinand and Isabella took Granada, the last Moorish stronghold in Spain. When the Arabs invaded Spain in 711, they drove the Christian forces north to the mountainous region of Asturias just south of the Pyrenees. In this frontier territory, the Spaniards built so many castles that it came to be known as Castile. As Christian kings and nobles began to push southward again, they built additional castles, often on the tops of hills, as at Peñafiel and Segovia (both p. 64), to control the plains and protect the cities below. Spanish castle architecture was influenced by Islamic designs, and such features as decorative masonry and elaborate battlements give many Spanish castles their characteristically Eastern appearance.

While northern Italy was nominally part of the Holy Roman Empire, the German emperors could exert control over much of it only when they were actually in Italy. During most periods, local Italian nobles, each with his own castle, dominated the countryside. Northern Italy was among the earliest areas in western Europe to see the revival of cities and the growth of long-distance trade and commerce. Venice and Genoa developed into major north Mediterranean seaports, while other Italian cities, such as Florence and Milan, became important manufacturers of such products as woolen goods and metalwork. The result was civic prosperity and power, accompanied by a great rise in urban population. In some cases, nobles moved into the cities; in

other cases, cities used their armed forces to conquer the surrounding countryside and forced local nobles to live within town walls. In the towns, Italian nobles built family compounds characterized by the same kinds of tall, usually rectangular towers they had built in the country. Such towers are recorded in cities as early as the beginning of the twelfth century. In Bologna there are said to have been some two hundred towers; one that has survived is more than 300 feet (91.4m) high. A number of these towers survive at San Gimignano (p. 67), and they continue to give the town a medieval appearance. After the death of the last Hohenstaufen emperor, Conrad IV (r.

1250–1254), northern Italy became, for all practical purposes, a collection of fully independent territories. During the fourteenth and fifteenth centuries, strongmen came to control many of the towns, and the larger towns expanded by conquering the smaller ones. The strongmen also had to protect themselves against rebellions by their subjects. In this atmosphere of almost constant warfare and intrigue, castles and town walls continued to be built for protection and to be updated as siegecraft became more and more sophisticated. Many late Italian castles were still built primarily for military purposes, though prestige and comfort were also important considerations.

Above: *The Château of Chinon (Indre-et-Loire) in central France is located on a hill above the town of Chinon and the river Vienne. Although the castle seems to present a single front more than a quarter of a mile (0.4km) long, it is actually three separate castles that were once separated by moats.*

The castle was begun by the counts of Blois at the end of the tenth century, and the oldest surviving section dates from the twelfth century, when King Henry II of England built the easternmost castle, Fort St.-Georges. Joan of Arc first met the Dauphin, the future Charles VII of France (r. 1422–1461), at Chinon Castle.

Right: The stone bridge at Chinon spans the former moat, now given over to lawns and gardens, between the Château du Milieu and the Fort St.-Georges. On the left of the bridge is the 108-foot-tall (32.9m) Clock Tower.

Left, bottom: The Château of Haut-Koenigsburg is located in the town of Haut-Koenigsburg, 10 miles (16km) north of Colmar (Bas-Rhin) in Alsace (northwestern France) in a frontier area that at various times has been part of both France and Germany. Built in the early twelfth century, the castle is situated on the top of a mountain almost 230 feet (70.1m) high; it was expanded over the next few hundred years. In 1462 the castle was largely destroyed, but was rebuilt soon after. In 1633, during the Thirty Years' War, Haut-Koenigsburg was set on fire, and it remained in ruins until it was reconstructed by Kaiser Wilhelm II of Germany (r. 1888–1918) in the early years of the twentieth century. Seen here are one of the corner towers and a stretch of an interior wall.

Left and below: Saumur (Maine-et-Loire) in central France is a town on the Loire near its confluence with the Thouet River. The Château was built in the eleventh century, had flanking towers added in the thirteenth century, was rebuilt in the fourteenth century, and was modernized in the sixteenth century. Note the stair turret (left) in the inner courtyard.

Above: The castle of Almodóvar del Rio, in Córdoba Province, southern Spain, was built by the Moors in 740 on the top of a 330-foot (100.6m) rocky hill. Captured by Ferdinand III of Castile (r. 1217–1252) in the thirteenth century after a four-year siege, the castle later fell into ruins and was restored at the beginning of the twentieth century.

Left: *Marked by its striking keep with decorative bands and hanging turrets, Fuensaldaña Castle, in Valladolid Province, north central Spain, was built in the mid-fifteenth century by the treasurer of King John II of Castile (r. 1406–1454), whose tower in the Alcazar of Segovia is characterized by similar turrets. The central keep, which is known as the* torre del homenaje *("tower of homage"), is a characteristic feature of Spanish castles.*

Right, top: Peñafiel Castle in Valladolid Province, Spain, was founded in the eleventh century and was rebuilt several times over the ensuing centuries. Much of the present castle dates from the early fourteenth century, though the tower was built in the mid-fifteenth century. Peñafiel, which runs along the crest of a hill, is a superb example of the type of Spanish castle called gran buque ("great ship"). It has a double defensive wall. *Right, bottom:* The Alcazar of Segovia, the capital of Segovia Province, central Spain, was built in the late eleventh century by King Alfonso VI of Castile (r. 1072–1109) on a site to the west of the town above the confluence of the Eresma and Clamores rivers. Alfonso based his castle in part on the Moorish Alcazar of Toledo. Rebuilt in the 1300s and expanded a century later, this castle was severely damaged by fire in 1862 but was restored later in the century.

Below: The town of San Marino is the capital of San Marino, a small independent republic near the Adriatic coast in east central Italy. The town is built on a mountain with three peaks—two crowned by towers, the third by a castle—linked by a walkway. The castle was probably begun in the eleventh century, but the present structure, surrounded by two sets of walls, dates largely from the fifteenth century and after.

Above: Built around 1400 for Archbishop Alfonso de Fuesca of Seville, the Castillo de Coca, in Segovia Province, central Spain, remained the property of the Fonseca family for many centuries. Built of brick with three sets of walls, Coca is a particularly fine example of the Mudejar (Moorish) style of architecture.

Right: Located in southern Italy 20 miles (32km) east of Aquila, in Abruzzi (formerly in Apulia), Castel del Monte was built around 1240 by the Hohenstaufen emperor Frederick II (r. 1197–1250, crowned 1220). It served in part as a hunting lodge where the emperor, a noted falconer, could fly his birds. Built on a luxurious scale, Castel del Monte was constructed in the form of an octagon with eight corner towers, also octagonal. It has been suggested that Frederick himself designed the castle.

Above: Located between Volterra and Florence in northern Italy, San Gimignano, Tuscany, is a town that still retains its medieval wall. It is marked by its medieval towers, thirteen of which have survived out of a total said to have originally numbered seventy-two. These towers were built by noble families and served as strongholds and refuges during feuds between families and during periods of urban strife. The tallest remaining tower is 174 feet (53m) high.

Right: The Castle of Fenis, in the Val d'Aosta in northern Italy, was built to guard a mountain pass. The castle is first mentioned in 1242 and was substantially modified from 1340 to the end of the fourteenth century. It is noted for the wall paintings in its chapel and great hall.

CHAPTER V

GERMANY, AUSTRIA, AND SWITZERLAND

Germany, as a state, was created in the ninth century. When Charlemagne's son, the emperor Louis the Pious, died in 840, the Frankish Empire was divided among Louis' three sons. The easternmost portion—most of which is part of Germany today—went to another Louis, thereafter known as "the German" (r. 840–876). Members of the Carolingian dynasty ruled Germany until 887, but following the deposition of Charles the Fat (r. 876–887), the monarchy became elective.

There were several major differences between Germany and France in the ninth and tenth centuries. While France broke down into many largely independent territorial units, Germany was marked by the establishment of five large duchies: Bavaria, Franconia, Saxony, Swabia, and Thuringia. In France, feudalism was the norm in many areas. In Germany, feudalism was not as fully developed, particularly in the east, where the royal army was still largely composed of freemen rather than armored knights. In Germany, the tradition of loyalty to the king was stronger than in France.

During the ninth century, Germany, like other areas in the West, was raided by Vikings. From the mid-ninth century on, a more serious threat was posed by the Magyars, wild horsemen who by the early tenth century were regularly attacking different parts of Germany on an almost yearly basis. In 919, following the reigns of two weak kings, German nobles decided they needed a strong ruler to defeat the Magyars, and they elected as king the most powerful of the German dukes, Henry the Fowler of Saxony (r. 919–936). Henry and his son Otto I "the Great" (r. 936–973, crowned 962) were able to defeat the Magyars, and Otto then set about strengthening royal power over the dukes. The Saxon, or Ottonian, kings based their power on freemen, on high churchmen, and on the *ministeriales*, a new class of serf-knights. The freemen provided military service; bishops and abbots were given land and governmental powers in return for administrative services and military support (they raised troops and sometimes even fought beside them); and the *ministeriales* served as armored cavalry and later as low-level admin-

Pages 70 and 71: Burg Eltz is situated on a rock 600 feet (182.9m) above the town of Moselkern, Rheinland-Pfalz, Germany, near the confluence of the Moselle and Eltz rivers. Built in the twelfth century, Eltz has been called the only perfectly preserved German castle. Burg Eltz is what is known as a Ganerbenburg, a castle with several different owners, each of whom has his or her own residence within the castle.

---

istrative officials. German kings were able to count on the loyalty of all three groups: the freemen by tradition, the churchmen because they were royal appointees, and the *ministeriales* because they could lose their freedom if they did not obey the kings. In 962, Otto I went to Rome and was crowned emperor, thus reviving what was later called the Holy Roman Empire.

During the ninth and tenth centuries, the Church everywhere—including the papacy—fell under lay control. Laymen appointed unqualified persons to church offices, sold the offices, or, on occasion, filled the offices themselves. From 910 on, a growing reform movement, associated with the monastery of Cluny, sought to end lay control. In the mid-eleventh century, this reform movement reached the papacy (which had been controlled largely by local Roman nobles) when Henry III of Germany (r. 1039–1056, crowned 1046) went to Rome to be crowned emperor and appointed a reform pope. Henry died in 1056, leaving his six-year-old son as heir. During Henry IV's

minority, the papacy was able to expand greatly its authority over the Church and to set up a papal election process that would free it from lay control. When Henry came of age, he found a newly strengthened papacy ready to challenge his control over the Church. Henry needed to be able to appoint bishops and abbots because they served as his administrative agents and supplied him with military support. However, Henry's rival in this battle for control over the Church, Pope Gregory VII (1073–1085), saw these men primarily as churchmen invested with spiritual powers who should therefore be free from any sort of lay control. The conflict came to focus on the ceremony in which churchmen were invested with the symbols of their office. The papacy opposed lay investiture, and the resulting conflict became known as the Investiture Controversy.

The Investiture Controversy (1076–1122) was accompanied by widespread local warfare in Germany. The main parties in this warfare were the emperors and the German nobles who, in opposition to imperial control, advanced candidates of their own for the crown—generally with papal support. Local conflicts and feuds also played a part in these divisions: if one of the local parties supported the emperor, the opposing faction would adhere to the nobles. The absence of any effective overall authority led to widespread anarchy and insecurity, and so to the rise of feudalism. Freemen became vassals of nobles or were forced into serfdom; the *ministeriales* threw off their serfdom and sold their services to the highest bidder; and as local nobles sought to protect themselves, castles sprang up everywhere. The period of the Investiture Controversy therefore marks both an important stage in the long-term loss of imperial control over Germany and the first great wave of German castle building.

During the twelfth and thirteenth centuries, several developments further reduced royal control in Germany. When Henry V of Germany (r. 1106–1125, crowned 1111) died in 1125 without leaving a direct heir, the monarchy once again became elective, and the nobles, always in favor of a weak king, chose Lothair II (r. 1125–1137, crowned 1133) of the Welf family, the weaker candidate. When Lothair died in 1137 without a direct heir, the nobles chose Conrad III (r. 1138–1152) of the rival Hohenstaufen family. The struggles between these two families led to what in effect were permanent rival parties. The Hohenstaufen usually (but not always) were the imperial party; the Welfs led the nobles, supported by the pope. In Italy, these parties were known as the Guelphs and the Ghibellines—the latter named from the Hohenstaufen castle of Waiblingen.

Under these circumstances, the emperors faced what amounted to a permanently organized opposition. When Emperor Frederick I Barbarossa (r. 1152–1190, crowned 1155) attempted to restore imperial control over northern Italy, therefore, he first had to make major concessions of political rights to German nobles to ensure peace in Germany while he was absent. Frederick failed in northern Italy, but did manage to marry his son, Henry VI of Germany (r. 1190–1197, crowned 1191), to the heiress to the Norman kingdom of Sicily and

South Italy. Henry died after a short reign, leaving a two-year-old heir, and a long period of civil war ensued. When Frederick II of Hohenstaufen came of age, he chose to base himself in his mother's kingdom of Sicily. To retain control in Germany, he made further concessions to the German nobility. When Frederick II's son Conrad IV (r. 1250–1254) died, the German monarchy became truly elective again, and German kings lost many of their remaining royal powers. Germany became a collection of virtually independent principalities, cities, and territories and continued as such into the nineteenth century.

Under these circumstances of insecurity, warfare, and absence of central control, castles continued to flourish. Some castles (e.g., Hohensalzburg, pp. 76–77) were built as refuges, others to control territory, and still others to command trade routes and prey (legally or illegally) on merchants and travelers. This last objective helps to explain the high concentration of castles along major rivers such as the Rhine (e.g., the Marksburg and Burg Stahleck, p. 74, and Rheinstein, p. 75) and the Moselle (Burg Eltz, pp. 70 and 71). During the

later Middle Ages and in the early modern period, Germany remained subject to warfare, and castle defenses were continually updated. At the same time, castles were rebuilt to make them more comfortable to live in. During the Religious Wars of the sixteenth and seventeenth centuries, many castles were destroyed, however, and the survival of German castles today is due largely to restoration during the nineteenth and twentieth centuries.

Austria was originally the German East March (Ostmark), the southeastern frontier of Germany. Austria remained within Germany and the German Confederation until 1866. The political background leading to the building of Austrian castles is very like that in the rest of Germany.

Initially Switzerland was also mainly German territory. In 1291 three cantons formed a defensive league, and during the fourteenth and fifteenth centuries other nearby cities and territories joined this Swiss Confederation. During the fifteenth century, there was much warfare in Switzerland, often quite brutal. Consequently, Swiss castles continued to be important militarily.

Right, top: The Marksburg, near Braubach, Rheinland-Pfalz, Germany, stands some 500 feet (152.4m) above the Rhine. The oldest surviving part of the castle dates from the twelfth century; the keep is thirteenth-century, the great hall fourteenth-century; and the chapel of St. Mark, from which the castle's name is derived, dates from 1437. Additions were made as late as the eighteenth century, and the older parts of the castle have been well restored.

Right, bottom: Built above the Rhine at Bacharach, Rheinland-Pfalz, Germany, Burg Stahleck was the main residence of the twelfth- and thirteenth-century Counts Palatine of the Rhine. The French destroyed much of the castle in the seventeenth century. *Opposite:* Rheinstein Castle, Rheinland-Pfalz, Germany, is located above the Rhine across from the village of Assmannshausen. Probably built in the thirteenth century, the castle belonged for a time to the archbishop-electors of Trier. Rheinstein was restored in the 1820s.

Above: The Wartburg, near Eisenach, Thuringia, Germany, was built in the late eleventh century, during the Investiture Controversy, by a landgrave of Thuringia. A famous contest between German minstrels took place here in 1207; this contest is the subject of Wagner's opera Tannhäuser. *The Wartburg was the home of Saint Elizabeth of Thuringia (1207–1231), who lived here later in the thirteenth century; in the sixteenth century, Martin Luther (1483–1546) completed his translation of the New Testament here. The present buildings date largely from the twelfth, thirteenth, and fourteenth centuries, and the castle was restored in the nineteenth century.* **Right:** *Built along a 400-foot (121.9m) hill above the city of Salzburg, Austria, Hohensalzburg was the former fortress of the archbishops of Salzburg. The castle was begun in 1077, at the beginning of the Investiture Controversy, as a refuge for the archbishop who supported Pope Gregory VII against the emperor. Over the next six centuries, many additions were made and remodelings undertaken, both for defensive purposes and for comfort. The staterooms of Hohensalzburg date mostly from the sixteenth century and are an excellent example of the late-medieval transformation of the castle interior to that of a great house.*

Opposite: Château l'Aigle, located in a wine-growing district of southeastern Switzerland near the French border, was built in either the eleventh or the twelfth century and belonged to the House of Savoy until its capture in the late fifteenth century by the soldiers of the Swiss town of Bern. The present castle dates mainly from that time.

Left, top: Chillon Castle was built on a rocky inlet near the eastern shore of Lake Geneva (Lac Léman), Switzerland, not far from Montreux. There was a castle here as early as the ninth century, built to protect one of the main roads to the Great St. Bernard pass to Italy, but the present castle was for the most part built by the counts of Savoy in the late twelfth and thirteenth centuries. During the sixteenth century, the castle was used as a state prison and was the setting of the English poet Byron's "The Prisoner of Chillon."

Left, bottom: Located above the town of Gruyères in western Switzerland, the Château of Gruyères was begun in the early eleventh century and largely rebuilt in the late fifteenth century. Gruyères is another good example of how castles were transformed into great houses. It was restored in the nineteenth century.

Above: Schloss Hallwill, located near Seengen, 5 miles (8km) southwest of Wohlen, in northern Switzerland, is a castle in two parts built in an artificial pond. Begun in the early twelfth century, the castle consists of two sections connected by a drawbridge (left). Note how the walls run straight into the water. Hallwill was restored early in the twentieth century.

Right: Schloss Tarasp is located in eastern Switzerland near the Austrian and Italian borders. The castle stands in a commanding position on a peak almost 5,000 feet (1,524m) high. The earliest castle may date from the eleventh century, but the present structure was built largely in the thirteenth century and rebuilt during the sixteenth and seventeenth centuries, when it was occupied by Austrian governors. Tarasp was restored at the beginning of the twentieth century.

Left: Habsburg Castle, sited in Habsburg, 5 miles (8km) southeast of Brugg, in northern Switzerland, was the original home of the imperial Habsburg dynasty, which later ruled Austria and Spain. The castle was begun in the early eleventh century. The original stone keep still stands; its battlements, however, are modern additions. Next to the keep is a tower house dating largely from the twelfth and thirteenth centuries. Only part of the castle has survived.

Northern Europe, Eastern Europe, and the Crusader Regions

In northern Europe, castles tended to cluster in Denmark and along the Baltic coast. In the far north, the difficult terrain itself provided protection, town walls protected the centers of population, and feudalism with its contentious nobles came late to the region. Most of the Scandinavian castles that survive today date from the sixteenth and seventeenth centuries.

Page 82: Egeskov Castle was built in the first half of the sixteenth century on an island in a lake 15 miles (24km) southwest of Nyborg on the large island of Funen, Denmark, between the mainland and the island of Sjaelland, on which Copenhagen is situated. Egeskov is an excellent example of a Renaissance castle that was built primarily for comfort and relied largely on its inaccessibility for protection. **Page 83:** *Situated on the coast in the middle of strategic Kalmar Sound, which separates Öland Island from the southeastern Swedish mainland, in the town of Kalmar, Kalmar Castle was built in the eleventh century as a stronghold against the Danes, who then occupied what is today southern Sweden. Most of Kalmar's surviving buildings date from the sixteenth century and were built by King Gustav I Vasa (r. 1523–1560) and his successors. Both castle and town were badly damaged in the Swedish-Danish wars of the sixteenth and seventeenth centuries; the castle was restored at the end of the nineteenth century.*

In eastern and central Europe and in the Balkans, castle building remained essential for the protection of both life and territory. Eastern Europe was a frontier area for many centuries. To the north, during the thirteenth and fourteenth centuries, the Crusading Order of the Teutonic Knights pushed the German frontier east at the expense of the native populations. In central Europe, the ruling dynasties of Bohemia and Slovakia built castles at strategic locations to protect their lands. In the Balkans, many castles were built during the fourteenth and fifteenth centuries as protection against the Ottoman Turks who gradually overran the entire peninsula.

The Crusades provided an important stimulus to castle building, not only in the Middle East, but also in Greece and on the Mediterranean islands. Soldiers of the First Crusade captured the city of Jerusalem in July 1099. Over the next forty-four years, Crusaders captured coastal towns and expanded their holdings in Palestine, Syria, and Lebanon. In these areas the Crusaders first took over and in some cases rebuilt Byzantine and Arabic fortifications, and later began to build castles of their own. The Crusader States not only were frontier areas, but also were highly feudalized, and each of the many territorial lords had his own castle. To defend the Holy Land, monastic orders of fighting knights were established: the Order of Saint John (Hospitalers) and the Order of the Temple (Templars) were founded early in the twelfth century, and the Teutonic Knights later in the century. These Crusading orders built or occupied such major castles as Krak des Chevaliers (p. 94) and Montfort, while existing castles were improved and strengthened as part of the defenses of various towns on the Mediterranean coast.

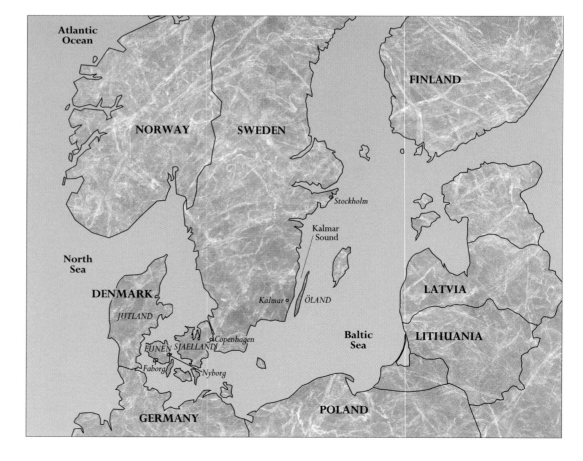

All these gains were only temporary, however. Most of the Crusading Kingdom of Jerusalem fell to Saladin in the 1180s. The remaining Crusader-held seaports in the Holy Land were captured during the thirteenth century, with the last port, Sidon, falling to Muslim forces in 1291. Frankish lords in Greece were replaced in time by Byzantines, Spaniards, and Italians, and by 1460 almost all of Greece had been conquered by the Ottomans. Both Cyprus and Rhodes fell to the Ottomans in the sixteenth century.

Unlike Europe, where castles continued to be occupied and modernized, many of the Crusading castles were abandoned. After they had ceased to serve their military use, even the largest castles, which had continued to be used as military bases after their capture, were vacated in favor of newly built, better located residences.

On his way to Acre, Israel, on the Third Crusade in 1191, Richard "the Lion Heart" captured the Mediterranean island of Cyprus. After the Fourth Crusade was diverted from its original objective of reconquering Jerusalem to the capture of Christian Constantinople in 1204, many of the Byzantine lands in Europe were occupied by Crusaders. These nobles (largely French) turned the conquered areas into lands held feudally from the loosely knit Latin Empire of Constantinople, and built western castles such as Mistra to control their territories. For a long time there was even a Frankish tower on the Acropolis in Athens. In 1309 the Hospitalers captured the island of Rhodes from the Byzantines and established their headquarters there.

Left: Marienburg (Malbork) Castle on the Nogat River some 25 miles (40.2km) southeast of Gdańsk, Poland, in what was formerly East Prussia, was begun in 1274 by the Order of the Teutonic Knights. In 1309, the Grand Master of the Order moved his headquarters here from Venice, and the upper castle and middle castle were completed during the fourteenth century; the outer walls date from the fourteenth and fifteenth centuries. The castle was restored in the early nine-teenth century. Marienburg was badly damaged in the last months of the Second World War, but has since been reconstructed.

Right: Situated on a hill near Brasov, Rumania, in an area of Transylvania that was formerly part of Hungary, Castle Bran was built by King Louis I of Hungary (r. 1342–1382) in 1377 to control the valley leading to Wallachia, with whose rulers the Hungarians were then at war. Count Dracula is said to have been imprisoned at Castle Bran during the fifteenth century. The castle remained an important strategic site during the era of Transylvanian independence in the sixteenth and seventeenth centuries, and was rebuilt in the seventeenth century.

Below: Located on the Berounka River nearly 20 miles (32km) southwest of Prague, in Bohemia, Czech Republic, Karlstein Castle was begun in 1348 by the emperor Charles IV (r. 1347–1378, crowned 1355), who was also King of Bohemia. In some respects, Karlstein is more like a palace than a castle. Charles built it to be a royal treasure house and the repository of the royal archives. The various churches and chapels within the castle are decorated with frescoes from the golden age of Bohemian painting. The Chapel of the Holy Cross, where the most important relics and the imperial crown were kept, has walls encrusted with semiprecious stones. Karlstein was restored in the late nineteenth century.

Above: Mistra Castle, on a mountain slope near Sparta in Greece, was begun by Guillaume II Villehardouin in the mid-thirteenth century after that Frankish noble had captured the last Byzantine stronghold in the Peloponnese. The castle was constructed in two parts: the lower castle lay along a ridge, and the upper castle, which could be reached only by narrow winding paths, was built above it. In 1259, Villehardouin was taken prisoner and had to surrender Mistra to the Byzantines as part of his ransom. In 1460, the castle was captured by the Turks.

Right, top: After the Hospitalers conquered the isle of Rhodes, Greece, in 1309, they began to reinforce the port's defenses, and continued this process as long as they held the island. Located in the town of Rhodes, the Fort of St. Nicola was built around 1460 on a small promontory at the edge of the harbor. The Fort of St. Nicola withstood several Turkish sieges, but in 1522 the Turks finally took the fort and conquered Rhodes.

Right, bottom: *The sea fort at Sidon, southern Lebanon. Although Saladin took Sidon in the 1190s, the town was restored in 1228 to the Franks, who rebuilt the defenses and added this new sea fort, which protected the entry to the port and was connected to the town by a bridge. The city of Sidon fell to the Turks in 1291, but remained an important commercial port; the castle was modified on a number of occasions before being badly damaged during a naval bombardment in 1840. The sea fort was restored in the twentieth century.*

A bove: *The ruins of Beaufort are situated on a high hill about 10 miles (16km) from Sidon in southern Lebanon, near the border with Israel. Originally an Arab castle, Beaufort was captured by the Franks in 1139, recaptured by the Arabs in 1190, ceded to the Franks in 1240, and reconquered by the Muslims in 1268. Each time Beaufort changed hands, its conquerors added to and improved the fortifications. Most of the surviving Crusader work is in the upper part of the castle.*

Right, **top:** *Located on a hilltop about 8 miles (12.8km) north of Telkalakh, Syria, just north of the Lebanese border, Krak des Chevaliers (Kerak) is one of the largest and best preserved of the Crusader castles. Built on the site of an earlier Arab castle, Krak was turned over to the Hospitalers in 1142. Over the next sixty years, Krak was damaged by three earthquakes; it was rebuilt and enlarged each time. The rebuilding of 1202 included the addition of the outer wall, which was almost 450 feet (137.2m) long on its west side. At one time, the castle was said to have housed two thousand residents. Krak fell to the Muslims in 1271 and continued to be used by them as a fortress for several hundred years. The castle has been under restoration since the 1920s.*

Right, bottom: *Interior view, Krak des Chevaliers.* **Opposite:** *Refectory of the Order of Saint John, Acre, Israel. This vaulted dining hall belongs to a building within the Hospitaler quarter in Acre that probably dates from the thirteenth century. Such halls were characteristic of a number of Crusader castles.*

CHAPTER **VII**

𝔓ALACES,
𝔚ALLED 𝔗OWNS,
AND
𝔐ODERN 𝔠ASTLES

As a general rule, nobles lived in castles, townsmen lived

behind the protection of town walls, and kings lived in

palaces; but the lines between these three kinds of fortifica-

tion could become blurred. Town walls might include sepa-

rate castles (as at Rhodes and Sidon, p.92), while the

difference between a castle and a palace was at times simply

one of scale—though technically speaking, a palace was

the official residence of a sovereign. The usual conception

of a palace, however, is of an elaborate and stately complex

of buildings—for example, Versailles, built by Louis XIV

(r. 1643–1715). The palaces considered here are elaborate

Page 91: Located 2 miles (3.2km) east of Fussen, Bavaria, Germany, almost on the Austrian border, Neuschwanstein Castle was built between 1869 and 1886 by King Ludwig II of Bavaria (r. 1864–1886) on the site of a medieval castle. The plan of Neuschwanstein was influenced by that of Wartburg Castle, and a theatrical designer worked on the original drawings. The interior contains many paintings by German Romantic artists depicting scenes from medieval history and Germanic legend. Page 97: The town of Ávila, the capital of Ávila province, central Spain, is noted for its eleventh-century walls, which are made of granite, are roughly a mile and a half (2.4km) long, and are reinforced by eighty-eight towers. These walls are the most complete surviving medieval town walls in Spain and are among the finest to be found in Europe.

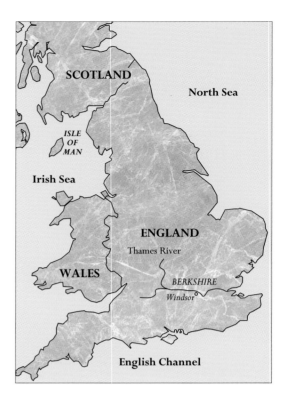

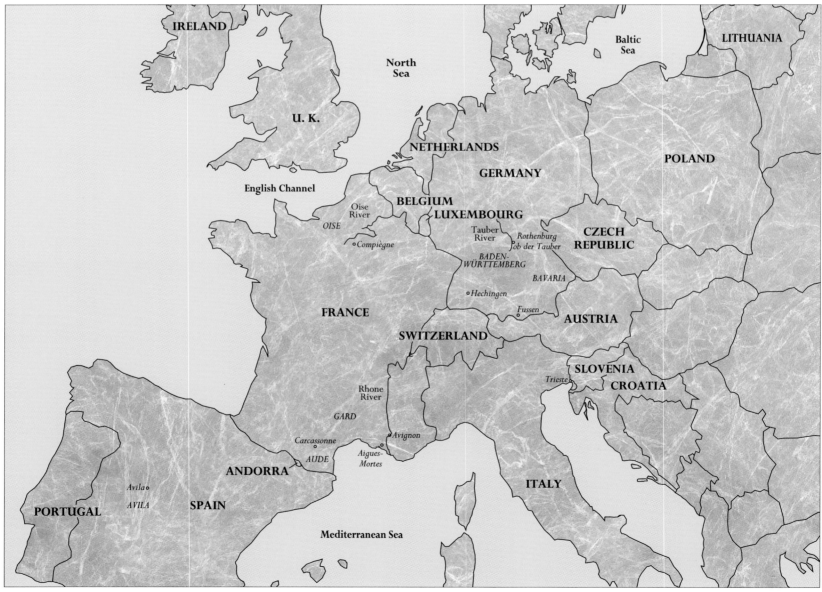

official residences that developed out of, or were associated with, castles.

During the eleventh and twelfth centuries, kings had many residences and traveled regularly between them, enabling the castles not occupied by the court to be cleaned and reprovisioned. From the late twelfth century on, a trend developed for kings (or at least for royal governments) to settle down in one place. Monarchs might continue to divide their time among castles, but there was a tendency to consider one of these a more formal, or sometimes an official, residence. In a period when castles were coming to be built for comfort as well as defense, the greater resources of kings enabled them to build far more elaborately than nobles could. The result was the palace.

Town walls go back to a time before historical records. During the Middle Ages, virtually all cities were fortified. In many cities extensions were built to earlier walls, or entirely new sets of walls were constructed as the population grew and areas outside the original walls were given protection. The word *suburb* literally means "under a city"; one may think of a suburb as a place under (that is, outside of) a city's walls. While medieval town walls were frequently extensive, very few have survived intact. As cities grew and warfare became less frequent, city walls became obstacles to transportation and were taken down. In many European cities, one can trace the lines of the old walls in the broad streets that have taken their place.

By the sixteenth century, as the need for fortification declined, castles in many parts of Europe were being turned into great houses. But in the eighteenth century, a new cultural movement, the Gothic Revival, developed in England and over the next two centuries spread to much of the rest of the world. One feature of this movement was building in medieval styles, and that led to the construction of entirely new castles and the rebuilding of old castles in the "Gothic" style. Even today, long after the Gothic Revival has ended, people continue to find a combination of nostalgia and magic in castles; and so, while new castles are largely limited to amusement parks, people continue to seek out and enjoy the old.

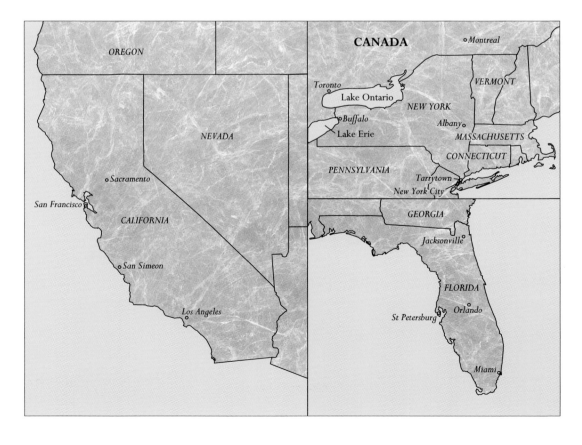

Right: Begun four years after the Battle of Hastings, Windsor Castle in the county of Berkshire, England, has remained the main royal residence of England. The oldest surviving part of the castle is the round tower (at far right), which dates from 1165 to 1179, though the upper half of the tower was added early in the nineteenth century. Today Windsor is a vast complex of buildings from many different periods. Shown here is the thirteenth-century Henry III Tower; the Tudor chimneys and television antenna are more recent additions.

Left: A French walled town on the Mediterranean, in the Rhone Delta, Aigues-Mortes (Gard) was founded by King Louis IX in 1246 as port of embarkation for his first crusade. The city was first defended by the 90-foot-high (27.4m) Tower of Constance, but Louis' son Philip III (r. 1270–1285) began the town wall in 1272. The rectangular walls, slightly more than a mile (1.6km) long, average 30 feet (9.1m) high and contain twenty towers and ten gates. The walls remain intact and have not been restored.

A *bove: Situated on the Rhone River in southern France, the Papal Palace at Avignon is a complex of buildings begun in 1316 after the popes had left Rome and settled in Avignon. Pope Benedict XII (1334–1342) remodeled and fortified the old bishop's palace, thus creating the Old Palace. His successor, Clement VI (1342–1352), began the New Palace, a more luxurious residence that was expanded by Clement's two successors. Both palaces are noted for the wall and ceiling paintings done by artists brought in from a number of European countries. The entire complex is surrounded by a powerful defensive wall marked by square stone towers. Avignon withstood sieges on several occasions in the fourteenth and fifteenth centuries.*

Left: Pierrefonds Castle near Compiègne (Oise), in northern France, was built by Louis of Orléans, the brother of King Charles VI of France (r. 1380–1422), shortly before the end of the fourteenth century. Pierrefonds is best known today because of its restoration, beginning in 1858, for Emperor Napoleon III (r. 1852–1870) by the French architect Viollet-le-Duc. For the emperor, the Middle Ages represented a period in French history characterized by the kind of glory he was trying to restore.

Above and opposite: Carcassone (Aude) in southern France is located on a strategic site overlooking the main road between the city of Toulouse and the Mediterranean Sea. The old city of Carcassone was built by the Romans and was occupied by the Visigoths in the fifth century. During the eleventh and twelfth centuries, Carcassone was ruled by the Trencavel family; early in the thirteenth century, the city was conquered by northern French forces. The famous walls of the Old City contain survivals from all these periods. The inner wall, started by the Visigoths on Roman foundations and added to by King Louis IX of France (r. 1226–1270) and his successors, has twenty-nine rounded towers. Within the inner walls is the castle built by the Trencavels in the twelfth century. The outer wall, which was built by Louis IX in the 1240s, contains seventeen towers and barbicans. Most of the outer towers were built with open sides facing the inner wall so that if taken the towers could not provide protection for the attackers. The walls were restored by the French architect Viollet-le-Duc in the mid-nineteenth century.

Right, top and bottom:
The Alhambra in Granada
in southern Spain has been
the site of a royal residence
since the eleventh century.
The oldest surviving part of
the Alhambra is the Alcazaba,
a thirteenth-century fortress
at the west end of the
Alhambra hill built when
Granada was the capital
of a Moorish kingdom. Next
to the Alcazaba is the
Alcazar, a magnificent
fourteenth-century palace
that is a masterpiece of
Spanish Islamic art charac-
terized by gardens with pools
and fountains and by
splendidly decorated rooms.
After the fall of Granada in
1492, the Catholic kings of
Spain built additional
palaces, churches, and other
structures onto the complex.
The whole is encircled by a
wall with many towers.

Above: Built on top of a 2,800-foot (853.4m) mountain above Hechingen in Baden-Württemberg, Germany, Burg Hohenzollern was probably built in the eleventh century, but was destroyed in 1423. It was rebuilt in the nineteenth century in Neo-Gothic style by Friedrich Wilhelm IV (r. 1840–1861) of the Hohenzollern dynasty. The only surviving part of the old castle is the fifteenth-century chapel.

*Above: Rothenburg ob der Tauber, Bavaria, southern Germany, is one of the best preserved medieval cities in Germany. The complete circuit of town walls includes part of the original twelfth-century wall as well as the new town wall, which was built in the fifteenth century. **Right:** The roofed sentry walk on the inner side of the wall.*

Above: *Miramar Castle, overlooking the Adriatic Sea near Trieste, Italy, was built between 1854* *and 1856 for Archduke Maximilian of Austria, who was Emperor of Mexico from 1864 to 1867.*

Left: The word kremlin *refers to the fortified citadel of a Russian city; it usually contains the residence of the ruler, his church or monastery, and other buildings. The Kremlin in Moscow, Russia, was the oldest part of that city, built in 1156 on high ground next to the Moscow River. In 1339 the Kremlin was expanded and surrounded by oak walls, but after a fire in 1365, the wooden walls were replaced with stone. From 1485 to 1495, Ivan III (r. 1462–1505) had a new brick wall built with notched battlements and gateway towers. This wall enclosed an area of some 70 acres (28ha). Within it are three cathedrals, several churches, and a number of palaces, all dating from the fourteenth to seventeenth centuries, in addition to various modern government buildings.*

Above: Situated on the Mediterranean between Haifa and Tel Aviv, Israel, the city of Caesarea was founded by the Phoenicians; it was later rebuilt by King Herod and was capital of the Roman province of Judaea. Caesarea was conquered by the Arabs in 640, captured by the Crusaders in 1101, taken by Saladin in 1187, and retaken by Richard the "Lion Heart" in 1191. In 1251, King Louis IX of France rebuilt the city wall. Louis' fortifications consisted of an outer wall some 15 feet (4.6m) high reinforced by sixteen towers, a 23-foot (7m) ditch, a 25-foot (7.6m) slope inclined at 60 degrees, and a 32-foot-high (9.8m) inner wall. Nevertheless, Caesarea fell to the Muslims in 1261 and was completely destroyed. Excavations of the site began in 1945 and have continued at intervals ever since.

*Above: Built by the
industrialist Sir Henry
Mill Pellatt between
1911 and 1914, the
spectacular Casa Loma,
located in Toronto, Ontario,
Canada, is North America's
largest castle.*

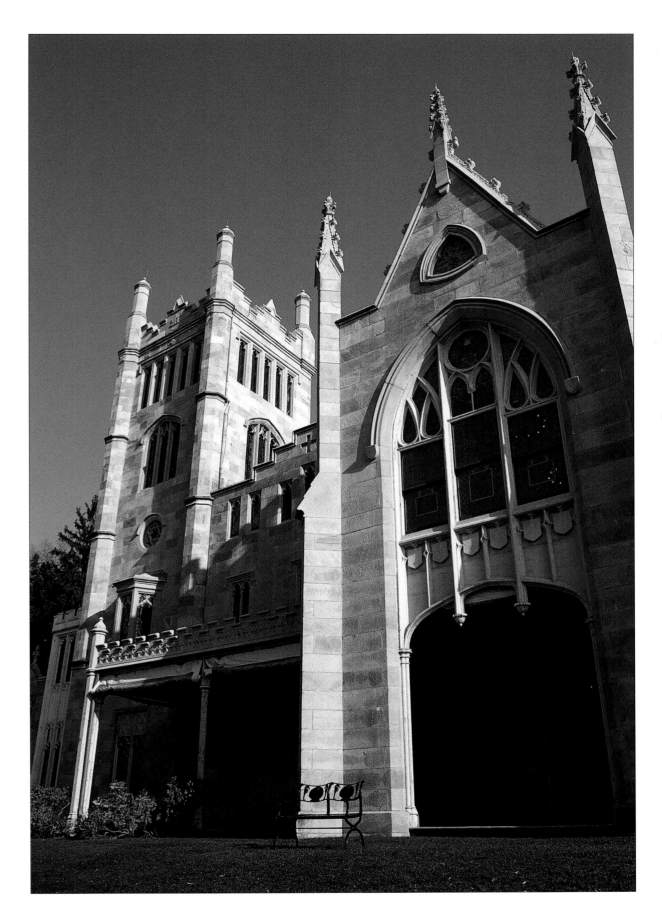

Left: An outstanding Gothic Revival mansion in Tarrytown, New York, U.S.A., Lyndhurst was designed in 1838 for General William Paulding by the American architect Alexander Jackson Davis (1803–1892). During 1864 and 1865, Davis added the tower and a dining room wing for Lyndhurst's second owner, George Merritt. The result was what has been called "a true Gothic castle," and the finest example of the Hudson River Gothic architectural style. Lyndhurst became the property of the National Trust for Historic Preservation in 1964 and has since been restored.

Right, top and bottom: Hearst Castle, at San Simeon, California, U.S.A., stands on the summit of a hill near the Pacific Ocean between San Francisco and Los Angeles. The complex was commissioned by publishing magnate William Randolph Hearst (1863–1951), and construction lasted from 1919 to 1945. After Hearst's death, the castle was given to the state of California. Hearst Castle has the commanding position of many medieval castles, but the architecture combines features from many periods. There are Spanish and Italian Renaissance buildings, Hispano-Moorish towers, a Graeco-Roman temple, and a mosaic from Pompeii, as well as a Gothic study, Gothic beds, medieval tapestries, and a collection of armor and other objects from the Middle Ages. Hearst Castle can be said to represent the idea of the castle carried to an extreme—or perhaps what results when an essentially European idea is transplanted to California.

Right: Cinderella Castle, Disney World, Orlando, Florida, U.S.A. This castle is the three-dimensional version of the prince's home in the movie Cinderella. Based on no particular historical castle, Cinderella is the castle that never was, but perhaps in our imagination always will be.

GLOSSARY

————◆◆————

adulterine castles: Castles built without royal permission when such permission was required.

arrow slits: Narrow openings in a wall through which defenders can fire arrows at attackers.

bailey: The outer courtyard of a castle; also, the wall surrounding that courtyard.

ballista: A kind of giant crossbow used to propel missiles.

barbican: An outer defensive work of a castle, often a heavily fortified gate tower.

battering ram: A heavy pole for knocking down gates, walls, etc. See illustration on page 13.

battlements: The notched top of a defensive wall.

castellan: The official in charge of a castle.

curtain wall: An exterior wall or a section of that wall between two gates or towers. Some castles had two sets of curtain walls.

donjon: A great tower in a castle; a keep.

garderobe: Here, a privy; toilet. The word is also used for a store-room or a private chamber.

keep: The strongest tower of a castle.

livery: A distinctive uniform worn by retainers.

mangonel: A siege engine in which a missile is held in a cup and fired by torsion. See illustration on page 12.

manor house: The estate house of a lord, built on a more modest scale than a castle.

moat: A ditch, usually filled with water, surrounding a castle. A common first line of defense.

motte: A high mound of earth on which a lord's residence is placed.

motte-and-bailey castle: An early form of castle; see page 11 for description.

palace: The official residence of a sovereign.

portcullis: A sliding iron grille used to block passage through a castle gate.

shell keep: An exterior ring of walls surrounding the crest of a motte.

siege: Surrounding and attacking a castle, usually a prolonged attack.

siege tower: A wooden tower brought up to a wall and used to climb onto the wall and thus gain access to a castle. See illustration on page 13.

solar: A private chamber on an upper floor lit by sunlight.

stockade: A timber wall or defensive barrier.

trebuchet: A sling powered by a counterweight.

turret: A small tower on the upper part of a castle, often placed at an angle in a castle wall.

ward: An open space within a castle's walls.

CASTLE SOCIETIES

————◆◆————

Europa Nostra, united with
  The International Castle
Institute
35 Lange Voorhout
NL - 2514 EC
The Hague, Netherlands

Ancient and Honourable
  Order of Small Castle Owners
  of Great Britain
c/o Hollis M. Baker
900 McKay Tower
Grand Rapids, MI 49503

BIBLIOGRAPHY

The Buildings of Ireland. Harmondsworth, Middlesex: Penguin, 1979–.

The Buildings of Wales. Harmondsworth, Middlesex: Penguin, 1979–.

Carreres, Carlos Sarthou. *Castillos de España.* Madrid: Espasa-Calpe, 1943.

Genicot, Luc F., ed. *Le grand livre des châteaux en Belgique.* Brussels: Vokaer, 1975–1977.

Le guide des châteaux de France. Rev. ed. Paris: Hermé, 1985–.

Hauswirth, Fritz. *Burgen und Schlosser der Schweiz.* Kreuzlingen, Switzerland: Gaissberg-Verlag, 1965–1970.

Holtz, Walter. *Kleine Kunstgeschichte der deutschen Burg.* 2d ed. Darmstadt, Germany: Wissenschaftliche Buchgesellschaft, 1972.

Kaufman, Edward, and Sharon Irish. *Medievalism: An Annotated Bibliography of Recent Research in the Architecture and Art of Britain and North America.* New York and London: Garland, 1988.

Kenyon, John R. *Castles, Town Defences, and Artillery Fortifications in Britain: A Bibliography 1945–74.* London: Council for British Archaeology, 1978.

_____. *Castles, Town Defences, and Artillery Fortifications in Britain and Ireland: A Bibliography.* London: Council for British Archaeology, 1983–.

King, David J. Cathcart. *Castellarium Anglicanum: An Index and Bibliography of the Castles in England, Wales, and the Islands.* Millwood, N.Y.: Kraus International, 1983.

Marconi, Paolo, et al. *I castelli, architettura e difesa del territorio tra medioevo e rinascimento.* Novara, Italy: Agostini, 1978.

Muller-Wiener, Wolfgang. *Castles of the Crusaders.* London: Thames and Hudson, 1966.

Pevsner, Nikolaus, gen. ed. *The Buildings of England.* Harmondsworth, Middlesex: Penguin, 1951–.

_____. *The Buildings of Scotland.* Harmondsworth, Middlesex: Penguin, 1978–.

Official handbooks for many British castles are available from Her Majesty's Stationery Office or at the castles.

ILLUSTRATION SOURCES

CHAPTER ONE, PAGE 9
Illustration of the Tower of London from the *Poems of Charles d'Orléans*, late 15th century (London: British Library, Royal MS. 16 F II, f.73).

CHAPTER ONE, PAGE 11
Illustration from the Bellifortis Manuscript, Italian, 15th century (Goettingen, Germany: Universitaetsbibliothek).

CHAPTER ONE, PAGE 11
Detail of the Bayeux Tapestry, English, c. 1067–1077 (Bayeux, Normandy: former Bishop's Palace).

CHAPTER ONE, PAGE 12
Illustration of a siege from the Manesse Manuscript, German, c. 1300–1340. Heidelberg, Germany: Univ. Bibl. Pal. Germ. 848, f. 229v.

CHAPTER ONE, PAGE 14
Illustration of cannon at a siege from the *Memoirs of Philippe de Commynes*, Rouen, France, 16th century.

CHAPTER TWO, PAGE 28
Illustration for the month of January from the *Grimani Breviary* (Flemish, c. 1480–1520, Venice: Biblioteca Marciana, MS. ss. f. lv.)

CHAPTER TWO, PAGE 29
The birth of Saint Edmund, from Lydgate, *The Life of St. Edmund*; Bury St. Edmund, after 1433 (London: British Library, Harley MS. 2278, f. 13v.)

INDEX

PHOTO CREDITS